BROOKE FRASER

COLLECTION

Exclusive Distributor for Australia & New Zealand:
Music Sales Pty. Limited
20 Resolution Drive
Caringbah NSW 2229, Australia

This book © Copyright 2007 by Wise Publications
ISBN: 1-921029-44-7
ISBN 13: 9 781921 02944 8
Order No. MS04137

Printed by Ligare Pty Limited
Design by Ben Lurie
Arrangements by Sean Peters
Photography Sophie Howarth

Wise Publications
Part of The Music Sales Group
London/NewYork/Sydney/Paris/Copenhagen/Madrid

Reprinted 2008
Reprinted 2009

CONTENTS

*selections from Albertine, all others from What To Do With Daylight

BROOKE FRASER
COLLECTION

Welcome to the official Brooke Fraser Collection. Whether you bought, borrowed, won or stole this music, I'm glad it's in your hands and hope it brings you many hours of pleasure. (NB: Stealing is bad. And if I'm doing my job right, by the end of playing these songs enough you'll have the urge to do the honest thing and go buy it.)

I was 19 years old when 'What To Do With Daylight' was first released in 2003, and five singles and an additional track from that initial offering are represented in this songbook. 'Albertine' is my most recent record, released in December 2006 (NZ) featuring songs written in the years subsequent to 'What to Do With Daylight' and stamped heavily with the subject matter I've been chewing over since then – justice, generations, purpose, eternity. This mental mastication I endeavour to express via accessible but artful melodies and interesting lyrics, that should propose and invite more than they do preach.

Think of them as the beginning of a conversation rather than a statement.

Your participation is invited. Let the dialogue begin.

Brooke Fraser

ALBERTINE

In 1994, the tiny Central-East African nation of Rwanda was devastated by genocide. Almost one million Rwandans were killed at the hands of their neighbours, friends and community leaders within the short space of 100 days... the catastrophic outcome of decades of tension and fighting between two ethnic groups – the Hutus and the Tutsis – a conflict that did not exist before Belgian colonists moved in during the first part of the 20th century and introduced an alien political divide.

My first visit to Rwanda occurred in June 2005, eleven years on from the atrocities. I visited local authorities, churches, schools, official memorials and living ones: child-headed households and communities living with AIDS, facing life without adequate medical care or basics like clean water. I met a people who are humble, joyous, diligent and in deep pain.

On the day before I was to fly out and onto Tanzania, my friend and guide Joel Nsengiyumva took me to a village school in a district called Kabuga. He wanted me to see that Rwanda had hope – and no better way to see it than in the next generation. The kids and I exchanged songs and dances, and as things wrapped up and we were about to leave, Joel asked if we could take a few minutes and meet with an orphan whose personal history he was familiar with.

Throughout my trip Joel had introduced me to people as a musician from the other side of the world who was going to go back to my people, tell them about the people of Rwanda and help. No pressure. That afternoon we walked across the schoolyard into an empty classroom, joined by a tall, beautiful girl wearing the school's cobalt and navy garb, where Joel's introduction was about to become a kind of commission.

Just before he shared her story with me, that of one person laying down their life for another, he uttered these words:

"You must go back to your people and you must write a song, and I will tell you what the name of the song is going to be."

He motioned toward the girl.

"This is Albertine."

Albertine is alive today because of the selfless, sacrificial love of another. Funny thing is, so am I. And now I want to know what it's like to love other people like that, so have decided to spend my whole life on the experiment.

Feel free to join me. We might just change the world.

ALBERTINE

Words and Music Brooke Fraser

Lyrics:
I am sit-ting still____ I think of An - gel- ique____

Her moth-er's voice o - ver me____ And the bul lets in the wall____ where it____ fell

ARITHMETIC

Words and Music Brooke Fraser

what to do — with day - light un-til I can make — you — mine —

You are the one — I want, — you are the one I want

I've been thinking of — changing my mind it ne-ver — stays the same for long

— but of all the things — I know for sure you're the — o - nly cer - tain one —

You are the one___ I want,___ you are the one___ I want

I've been

count-ing up all my wrongs one___ sor-ry for each star___ See I'd a-

still be the one ___ I ___ want ___ You'll still be the one ___ I want ___ You'll

still be the one ___ I ___ want

BETTER

Words and Music Brooke Fraser

Brooke plays this song with a capo on the third fret so
F becomes Ab, Am7 becomes Cm7, C becomes Eb etc.

C.S.LEWIS SONG

WORDS AND MUSIC BROOKE FRASER

26

27

DECIPHERING ME

Words and Music Brooke Fraser

We___ be long.___

Your te‐le‐scope eyes___ see ev‐'ry‐thing clear ‐ ly___

My vis‐ion is blurred___ but I know what I___ heard ech‐o ing___ all a round.___

While I___ am tun‐ing you in___ you are de‐ci ‐ pher ing___ me.___

(We__ be__long)   Oh   did you see the stars   col - li - ding?   Shin-ing just to show,

We_____   be - long.__

HYMN

WORDS AND MUSIC BROOKE FRASER

LIFELINE

WORDS AND MUSIC BROOKE FRASER

Brooke plays this song with a capo on the first fret
so Em becomes Fm, C becomes Db, D becomes Eb etc.

LOVE, WHERE IS YOUR FIRE?

Words and Music Brooke Fraser

Lyrics:

Love, where is your fi-re? I've been sit-ting here smo-king a way.

Mak ing sig-nals with sticks and odd ends and bits, but still there's no

47

rit.

SAVING THE WORLD

Words and Music Brooke Fraser

53

SCARLET

Words and Music Brooke Fraser

SHADOWFEET

Words and Music Brooke Fraser

WITHOUT YOU

WORDS AND MUSIC BROOKE FRASER